More Common Sense

Why the Home Should Not Be Collateral for Government Finance

Jim Hopson

Copyright @ 2026 Jim Hopson

All rights reserved.

No part of this book may be reproduced or transmitted in any form or by any means.

Published by Foundation Press

Author's Note

This book was not written out of ideology or frustration with any particular institution. It was written out of observation.

Over many years of working with homeowners, property records, and tax systems, I began noticing a pattern that didn't sit right. The questions people asked were reasonable. The confusion they felt was understandable. And the answers they were given rarely addressed what was actually happening.

Owner-occupied homes were being spoken about as though they were interchangeable with the property tax system itself. Shelter was treated as a revenue source rather than a foundation. Stability was managed rather than protected.

None of this appeared accidental.

The more I looked, the clearer it became that the system had drifted—quietly, incrementally, and without a clear moment of acknowledgment. What also became clear is that protecting the home does not weaken government. It strengthens the communities government depends on to function.

This book is an attempt to name that drift honestly and examine its consequences without exaggeration or anger.

I do not claim that reform is simple, painless, or immediate. I do claim that clarity matters. Systems cannot be corrected if they are not accurately described. And ownership cannot remain meaningful if its defining characteristics are slowly eroded without discussion.

This book does not argue against public services, shared responsibility, or government itself. It argues for alignment. It asks whether the home—the place where people live, plan, and anchor their lives—should function as collateral for obligations they cannot control.

That question deserves to be asked plainly.

My hope is that readers come away not with certainty about every solution, but with a clearer understanding of what is already happening—and with the confidence to insist that foundational assets remain foundational.

Table of Contents

The Home at the Center of the System 1
How We Got Here: Property, Power, and Purpose 7
Who Does What—and Why the System Never Changes 12
Why Fixing the Process Never Fixes the Problem 17
What the Homeowner Experiences in Real Life 21
Fee Simple Title, Collateral, and the Hidden Contract 25
When the Foundation Weakens, Everything Above It Shakes 29
Why the Middle Class Always Pays First 32
Why Alternatives Are Always "Impossible" 35
Where Real Change Actually Happens 38
Why a 100 Percent Exemption Is Not Radical 41
The Slow Shift No One Is Watching 45
The Objections That Always Appear—and Why They Fail 48
Responsibility, Citizenship, and the Long View 51
What We Are Really Deciding 54

The Home at the Center of the System

Most people buy a home believing they understand what they are getting into. They review the purchase price, sign a mortgage, secure insurance, and estimate monthly payments. The numbers are discussed, explained, and repeated until they feel familiar enough to accept. By the time closing arrives, everything appears to be accounted for.

And yet, one of the most consequential obligations tied to homeownership rarely receives the same level of attention.

Property taxes are usually treated as background noise. They are estimated rather than examined, bundled into escrow, and described as unavoidable. Buyers are told they will change, that they tend to go up, and that this is simply part of owning a home. Few are encouraged to ask deeper questions about how they work, why they exist in their current form, or what they imply over time.

This book begins with those questions.

Homeownership occupies a unique place in American life. It is not merely a housing choice. It is a social and economic anchor. A home provides shelter, stability, and continuity. It is where families are raised, where workdays begin and end, and where long-term plans quietly take shape. The idea of owning a home is deeply connected to independence, security, and personal freedom.

These ideas did not arise by accident. They are rooted in centuries of legal and cultural understanding about what it means to own property.

In the United States, ownership of real property is most often held in what is known as fee simple title. Fee simple represents the most complete form of ownership recognized by law. It conveys the right to possess, use, enjoy, and transfer property indefinitely. It is not temporary, and it is not meant to expire. At its core, it is intended to be permanent.

Fee simple title carries with it an implicit promise. That promise is not freedom from obligation, but security. The owner is meant to have a stable claim that cannot be casually revoked. This stability mattered. It allowed people to establish roots, build wealth gradually, and participate fully in civic life without constant fear of displacement.

The home, held in fee simple, was never meant to be fragile.

Yet in practice, modern homeownership has become increasingly conditional. Not through dramatic confiscation or sweeping policy announcements, but through a quiet, persistent mechanism that most homeowners are encouraged not to examine too closely.

That mechanism is the property tax.

Property taxes differ from other forms of taxation in an important way. Income taxes rise and fall with earnings. Sales taxes depend on consumption. Fees are tied to specific services or uses. Property taxes, by contrast, are imposed simply because a person owns and occupies land and shelter.

When property taxes are based on market value, the obligation grows as values rise, regardless of whether the homeowner's income has increased. This distinction matters. It means the cost of remaining in one's home is increasingly driven by forces outside the household.

Market appreciation may feel reassuring on paper, but it does not generate cash for the homeowner who lives in the property. It does not raise wages. It does not make monthly bills easier to pay. Yet it directly increases the tax obligation tied to ownership.

This is where the nature of ownership begins to shift.

A home subject to perpetual revaluation and escalating taxation functions not only as shelter, but as collateral.

Collateral is a familiar concept in lending. It is the asset pledged to secure repayment. If the obligation is not met, the asset can be taken. In the context of property taxation, the owner-occupied home is implicitly pledged as security for government revenue.

This pledge is not negotiated annually. It does not account for income, employment stability, health, or family circumstance. It exists automatically by virtue of ownership. Failure to meet the obligation leads to penalties, interest, and eventually the loss of the property itself.

The homeowner becomes, in effect, a co-signer on a growing public obligation.

Most homeowners do not experience this reality immediately. Early on, taxes feel manageable. Escrow absorbs the increases. Adjustments appear incremental. The system seems stable enough.

Over time, however, the pressure becomes harder to ignore. As values rise faster than income, margins narrow. Homeowners adapt. Discretionary spending is reduced. Maintenance is deferred. Savings are sacrificed. Appeals are filed. Exemptions are pursued.

These responses are rational. They are also defensive.

What began as ownership starts to feel conditional. The home remains occupied, but the sense of permanence weakens. The homeowner is no longer simply living in a place. They are managing exposure.

This experience is not limited to any one region or income level. It affects homeowners in cities and rural communities alike. It affects working families, retirees, and professionals. The common factor is not irresponsibility, but structure.

The property tax system did not emerge from malicious intent. It evolved as local governments sought reliable funding sources. Property proved attractive because it is visible, immobile, and difficult to avoid. As public responsibilities expanded, reliance on property taxation deepened.

Reliability for institutions, however, came at the cost of predictability for households.

A system that treats shelter as a dependable revenue source necessarily shifts risk onto those who occupy it. When values rise due to market forces, homeowners absorb the cost even if their financial capacity does not change.

This transfer of risk is rarely described in these terms. Property taxes are often defended as fair because they are applied uniformly. But uniform application does not guarantee equitable outcomes.

Taxing unrealized appreciation assumes liquidity where none exists. It treats shelter as a financial instrument rather than a necessity. That assumption conflicts with the original purpose of fee simple ownership.

Fee simple was meant to provide stability. It was intended to protect individuals from arbitrary loss and to support long-term independence. When the home becomes collateral for revenue growth, that stability erodes.

The homeowner is still called an owner, but ownership begins to resemble conditional tenure. The right to remain depends on the ability to absorb ongoing valuation-based obligations.

The consequences extend beyond individual households.

Stable homes support stable work. Stable work supports consistent income. Consistent income supports consumption, savings, and civic participation. When housing stability weakens, these relationships strain.

Homeowners facing unpredictable costs become more cautious. They delay career changes. They postpone entrepreneurship. They avoid long-term commitments. Communities experience higher turnover. Schools lose continuity. Local economies absorb uncertainty.

These effects accumulate quietly. They do not produce immediate crisis, which is why they persist. Over time, however, they weaken the very base upon which public services depend.

The homeowner is not peripheral to the system. The homeowner is central. The person who rises each morning, produces value, and returns home at night is the engine that funds everything else. Income taxes, sales taxes, and economic activity all flow from that stability.

When the home is destabilized, the system begins consuming its own foundation.

Understanding this does not require rejecting government or shared responsibility. It requires distinguishing between necessary funding and misaligned mechanisms.

Taxation itself is not the problem. It is a shared obligation that supports shared needs. The question is not whether government should be funded, but how.

Shelter occupies a unique category. It is not a luxury. It is not an income-producing asset for the person who lives in it. It is a prerequisite for participation in society. Treating it as collateral for revenue growth changes its role in fundamental ways.

Most homeowners never explicitly consent to this arrangement. They inherit it. It is embedded in the system they enter when they buy a home. Its consequences reveal themselves slowly, often long after the decision feels irreversible.

This book does not begin by assigning blame. It begins by clarifying reality.

Clarity changes the conversation. It shifts attention away from annual tax bills and toward structural alignment. It reframes property taxation not as a technical detail, but as a question of how ownership is defined and protected.

The chapters that follow examine how the property tax system developed, how authority is distributed, and why reform efforts focused solely on administration repeatedly fall short. They also explore an alternative approach grounded in the original promise of ownership.

That alternative rests on a simple premise: an owner-occupied home should not function as collateral for government growth. Shelter should be protected as a foundation, not leveraged as a revenue instrument.

Before that premise can be evaluated, the system itself must be understood. That understanding begins with history, authority, and purpose.

The next chapter turns to those origins and asks how a system built for a different era came to exert such powerful influence over modern homeownership.

How We Got Here: Property, Power, and Purpose

To understand how the owner-occupied home became exposed to perpetual taxation, it helps to step back from modern mechanics and look at origins. Systems rarely begin in their most complex or misaligned form. They evolve gradually, shaped by necessity, convenience, and habit. What feels inevitable in the present often began as a practical solution to a very different set of problems.

Property taxation is no exception.

In its earliest forms, taxing land was straightforward. Land was visible. It was difficult to hide. It was often the primary source of wealth. Governments with limited administrative capacity relied on what they could easily identify and assess, and land fit that requirement well.

In agrarian societies, land ownership often correlated directly with productive capacity. Crops were grown, livestock was raised, and income flowed from the land itself. Taxing land roughly approximated taxing economic output. The connection between ownership and income was clear, and the obligation felt proportionate.

This relationship made sense in its time.

As societies industrialized and diversified, that connection began to weaken. Wage labor expanded. Commerce grew. Services replaced agriculture as the dominant driver of economic activity. Wealth increasingly came from work, enterprise, and innovation rather than from land alone.

Tax systems adapted, but not evenly.

Income taxes emerged to capture earnings. Sales taxes followed consumption. Corporate taxes targeted enterprise. Yet property taxes persisted, especially at the local level, because they remained administratively simple and politically reliable.

Local governments discovered something important: property tax revenue was stable.

Property does not relocate easily. Owners cannot conceal it. Payment can be enforced through liens and, eventually, seizure. From a funding perspective, this reliability was powerful. Over time, reliance on property taxation deepened.

As local responsibilities expanded—particularly in education, infrastructure, and public safety—governments needed predictable revenue streams. Property taxes met that need. What began as a practical solution gradually became a structural pillar.

At this stage, a critical shift occurred.

The object of taxation was no longer land as a productive asset, but land and shelter as a place of residence. The owner-occupied home entered the tax base not because it generated income, but simply because it existed.

This shift was subtle. It was rarely debated openly. It felt natural because the tax was already there. What changed was scale and dependence.

Market value assessment accelerated that change.

As appraisal methods improved, governments gained the ability to capture appreciation with increasing precision. Rising values expanded the tax base without the need to raise rates explicitly. Revenue grew quietly. Budgets expanded with far less political friction than overt tax increases would have produced.

From an institutional standpoint, this was highly effective.

From a homeowner's standpoint, it introduced a new form of exposure.

The tax obligation was no longer loosely tied to productive use or income. It became tied to market perception. A home's value could rise because of regional growth, external investment, or speculative demand. The homeowner's obligation rose alongside it, regardless of whether their personal circumstances had changed.

This development was not framed as a change in ownership rights. It was framed as modernization. Better data. Fairer assessments. More uniform application.

Yet beneath these improvements was a deeper transformation.

Ownership was becoming less about permanence and more about compliance.

Fee simple title remained intact in name. The homeowner still held the deed. The rights to possess, use, and transfer the property remained. What changed was the condition of continued possession.

Failure to meet rising tax obligations carried consequences that were not merely financial. Penalties accumulated. Interest compounded. Liens attached. Ultimately, ownership could be lost.

This mechanism did not require intent. It operated automatically.

In effect, the home became collateral for public finance.

Collateralization through taxation differs in important ways from voluntary pledging through lending. In lending, the borrower agrees to the terms, understands the risk, and receives capital in exchange. In property taxation, the homeowner receives no new benefit when obligations increase. The pledge exists simply because the home exists.

That distinction matters, because it alters the character of ownership itself.

Historically, property rights were protected precisely to prevent arbitrary loss. Ownership was meant to secure independence from shifting political and economic pressures. The home was a refuge from uncertainty, not a conduit for it.

As property taxation expanded in scope and intensity, that protective role weakened.

The homeowner became exposed to forces far beyond their control. Market volatility entered the household through the tax bill.

Government growth became linked, however indirectly, to household vulnerability.

This linkage was rarely articulated openly. It was embedded in budgets, statutes, and administrative practice. Over time, it became normalized.

Normalization does not mean correctness. It means repetition.

Once a system becomes normalized, its assumptions are rarely questioned. Debate shifts toward refinement rather than reconsideration. Accuracy. Efficiency. Transparency. These discussions all take place within the existing framework, rather than challenging whether the framework itself still makes sense.

This is why reform efforts so often disappoint.

Homeowners are encouraged to engage through appeals, exemptions, and hearings. These tools address individual outcomes but leave the underlying structure intact. They assume the legitimacy of taxing shelter and focus on managing its effects rather than questioning its role.

The division of authority reinforces this pattern.

Appraisal offices determine value but do not set tax policy. Taxing entities set rates but do not define the tax base. Collectors enforce payment but do not create the obligation. Each actor operates within narrow bounds.

No single participant is positioned to reconsider the system as a whole.

Responsibility diffuses. Accountability blurs. Homeowners feel pressure but struggle to identify where meaningful change could occur.

For many years, this arrangement remained tolerable. Appreciation was slower. Incomes generally grew. Margins existed. The system's misalignment remained mostly hidden.

That balance has shifted.

In modern housing markets, appreciation can outpace income for long periods. Wage growth lags. Costs rise. The tax obligation compounds. What was once a background expense becomes a defining factor in household stability.

This shift exposes the tension at the heart of the system. A funding mechanism designed for reliability has become misaligned with the lived reality of ownership.

The original purpose of property rights was to secure independence. The modern application of property taxation increasingly undermines that security.

This is not an indictment of local government or public service. It is an acknowledgment that systems built for one era can outlive their alignment with another.

Understanding how we arrived here reframes the debate. The issue is not whether property taxes are legal. They are. It is not whether they fund necessary services. They do.

The issue is whether taxing owner-occupied homes based on market value remains consistent with the purpose of ownership itself.

Fee simple title was never intended to function as a revolving guarantee for public finance. It was meant to provide a stable platform from which individuals could work, contribute, and participate.

When that platform becomes unstable, the consequences extend far beyond the tax bill.

History shows that systems change not when they are exposed as flawed, but when their misalignment becomes impossible to ignore. The chapters that follow examine why attempts to fix the current system from within continue to fall short—and why structural reconsideration has become unavoidable.

Who Does What—and Why the System Never Changes

For most homeowners, the property tax system appears to operate as a single, unified process. A value is determined, a bill arrives, and payment is required. When that payment becomes difficult, frustration naturally follows. The homeowner looks for someone to question, challenge, or persuade.

What many do not realize is that the system they are engaging with is intentionally fragmented.

This fragmentation is not an accident. It is a design feature.

Responsibility within the property tax system is divided among multiple entities, each with a narrow role and limited authority. This division is often described as a safeguard against abuse or overreach. In practice, it also makes structural change extraordinarily difficult.

Understanding this division matters because it explains why homeowners can engage for years without altering the system's trajectory.

The first point of contact is usually the appraisal authority. Appraisal offices are responsible for determining taxable value. They collect sales data, apply valuation models, and issue notices. Their work is technical and procedural. They are tasked with applying the law as written, not questioning whether that law still makes sense.

Appraisal offices do not decide what types of property should be taxed. They do not determine how much revenue must be raised. They do not control tax rates. Their authority ends with valuation.

This limitation is often misunderstood.

When homeowners challenge an appraisal, they are engaging with a process designed to defend methodology, not reconsider structure. Even when an appraisal office acknowledges an error, the correction is confined to the individual account. The broader system remains untouched.

Accuracy at the appraisal level does not resolve exposure. It simply recalculates it.

The next participants are the taxing entities themselves. Cities, counties, school districts, and special districts set tax rates based on approved budgets. Their role is financial, not philosophical. They are responsible for funding obligations that already exist.

Those obligations are real and immediate. Payroll must be met. Debt must be serviced. Contracts must be honored. Statutory duties must be fulfilled. As a result, rate setting is driven by necessity more than discretion.

Taxing entities do not determine property values, nor do they define what belongs in the tax base. They operate within a framework established by the state. When revenues fall short, rates adjust. When values rise, rates may remain unchanged while revenue increases.

This mechanism allows budgets to expand without the visibility of a formal rate increase. From the public's perspective, this feels subtle. From the homeowner's perspective, it often feels disingenuous.

The third participant is the tax collector. Collectors issue bills, receive payments, and enforce compliance. Their authority is entirely administrative. They do not influence valuation, rate setting, or policy. They implement outcomes determined elsewhere.

Collectors represent the most tangible point of pressure for homeowners. Penalties, interest, and enforcement actions are immediate and concrete. Yet collectors are enforcing obligations they neither designed nor can modify.

This division of labor produces a predictable result.

Each participant can accurately claim limited authority. Appraisers apply statutes. Taxing entities fund obligations. Collectors enforce the law. No single actor is positioned to reconsider whether the system itself remains appropriate.

Responsibility exists everywhere and nowhere at the same time.

For homeowners, this fragmentation produces exhaustion. Engagement becomes cyclical. A protest may reduce a value temporarily. A hearing may influence a rate marginally. The following year, the process begins again.

Nothing structural changes.

This outcome is not accidental. Fragmentation insulates the system from direct challenge. Pressure applied at one point is absorbed without transmitting force to the whole.

Appeals correct errors without questioning premise. Hearings allow participation without altering design. Transparency explains outcomes without changing obligation.

The system remains intact.

This design evolved for practical reasons. Dividing authority reduces political risk. It prevents any single office from becoming the sole target of frustration. It also stabilizes revenue by making abrupt change difficult.

Stability for institutions, however, does not guarantee alignment for households.

As discussed in earlier chapters, the burden imposed by valuation-based taxation has grown steadily over time. In many markets, appreciation now outpaces income growth for long periods. What was once manageable has become destabilizing for a growing number of homeowners.

Yet the structure of the system prevents that pressure from being addressed directly.

Appraisal offices can refine models, but they cannot remove shelter from the tax base. Taxing entities can adjust rates, but they cannot redefine taxable property. Collectors can enforce payment, but they cannot reconsider obligation.

Each part functions as designed. The problem is not malfunction. The problem is misalignment.

This misalignment becomes especially clear when homeowners attempt to advocate for change.

Local engagement is encouraged because it is visible and accessible. Homeowners attend city council meetings, school board hearings, and appraisal review boards. They voice concerns and request relief.

These forums can produce incremental adjustments. They cannot produce structural reform.

The authority to define what is taxable rests at the state level.

States establish property tax frameworks. They define exemptions. They allocate authority. They determine whether owner-occupied homes are included in the tax base and under what conditions.

This distinction is critical. It determines where meaningful change is possible.

When homeowners focus exclusively on local actors, effort is often misdirected. Local officials may sympathize but lack authority. Administrative improvements may occur, but exposure remains.

The system absorbs dissatisfaction without altering direction.

This explains why reform efforts that stay inside the existing framework so often disappoint. The tools provided to homeowners are defensive rather than transformative. They allow individuals to manage risk, but not eliminate it.

Understanding this reality changes the posture of engagement.

The homeowner is not merely a participant in an annual process. The homeowner is a stakeholder in how ownership itself is defined and protected. That stake cannot be exercised fully through appeals or hearings alone.

Recognizing where authority resides does not diminish the value of local participation. It places it in context. Appeals remain useful. Hearings remain important. They are not solutions to a structural problem.

The chapters that follow examine what happens when reform efforts focus exclusively on administration and why those efforts repeatedly fall short. They also begin to outline what meaningful structural reconsideration would require.

Change does not begin with better paperwork. It begins with confronting design.

Why Fixing the Process Never Fixes the Problem

Once homeowners begin to understand how the property tax system is structured, a natural question follows. If the system is misaligned, why has so much energy been devoted to fixing the process rather than reconsidering the design?

The answer is not indifference. It is incentive.

Most reform efforts focus on administration because administration is manageable. Procedures can be adjusted. Timelines can be clarified. Notices can be rewritten. Appeals can be refined. Each change is presented as progress, and in narrow ways, each one is.

None of them alters the underlying exposure faced by the homeowner.

Process reform assumes that the system itself is sound and that problems arise from execution. If values are inaccurate, make them more accurate. If communication is unclear, make it clearer. If hearings feel unfair, make them more orderly.

These improvements matter at the margins. They do not change the nature of the obligation.

A precisely calculated burden based on a misaligned premise remains misaligned. Accuracy does not create stability. Clarity does not reduce exposure.

This helps explain why homeowners often feel better informed but no more secure after engaging with reform initiatives. The system becomes easier to understand without becoming easier to live with.

Valuation accuracy provides a clear example. Appraisal methods have grown increasingly sophisticated. Data sets are larger.

Models are more precise. Assessments are more defensible than ever.

For the homeowner, greater accuracy often means higher taxes. When market values rise, precision ensures that increases are captured efficiently. The issue is not error. It is linkage.

When shelter is tied directly to market valuation, improved precision amplifies pressure rather than relieving it.

Transparency reforms follow a similar pattern. Homeowners are given clearer explanations of how values are calculated and how rates are set. Access to information improves. Educational materials expand.

Understanding how the system works does not make the outcome affordable. In many cases, transparency heightens frustration. The clearer the explanation, the more obvious the limitation becomes.

Appeals are frequently cited as proof of fairness. Homeowners are told they have a right to challenge their valuation and present evidence. In theory, this provides a safeguard.

In practice, appeals are reactive and individualized. Relief depends on time, persistence, and familiarity with process. Even when successful, appeals address only a single year.

Exposure remains.

Caps and exemptions are often offered as compromise solutions. They soften the impact of rising values without redefining the tax base. These measures provide temporary relief and political cover.

They also add complexity.

Over time, layered caps and exemptions create systems that are difficult to explain and uneven in effect. Long-term owners are treated differently from new buyers. Some households benefit more than others based on timing rather than circumstance.

Most importantly, these measures do not eliminate exposure. They slow it.

Slowing an unsustainable trajectory does not make it sustainable. It simply delays the point at which pressure becomes unavoidable.

The persistence of process-focused reform is not accidental. Administrative changes preserve revenue stability. They avoid uncomfortable conversations about funding alternatives. They allow systems to adapt without confronting their underlying assumptions.

Structural reform, by contrast, introduces uncertainty. Removing owner-occupied homes from the tax base forces governments to examine how services will be funded without automatic growth tied to appreciation. That examination is politically difficult and fiscally demanding.

As a result, reform energy is directed toward what feels achievable rather than what is necessary.

This pattern explains reform fatigue. Homeowners are encouraged to engage year after year in processes that never resolve the central issue. Participation becomes an obligation rather than a path to stability.

The system absorbs dissatisfaction without changing direction.

From an institutional perspective, this adaptability is a strength. From a household perspective, it is exhausting.

The deeper issue is that process reform treats symptoms rather than causes. Rising tax pressure is managed as a technical problem instead of acknowledged as a design choice. The assumption that shelter should be taxed based on market value is left largely unexamined.

That assumption deserves scrutiny.

Owner-occupied homes do not generate income for the people who live in them. They are not discretionary consumption. They are not speculative assets for most households. Treating them as a revenue source equivalent to income-producing property ignores these distinctions.

No amount of procedural refinement can reconcile that mismatch.

This is why reform efforts confined to administration consistently fall short. They are constrained by the same assumptions that create instability. They cannot deliver predictability because predictability was never the system's primary objective.

The objective was reliability.

Recognizing this does not diminish the value of process improvements. Appeals, transparency, and administrative fairness remain necessary.

They are not sufficient.

They can make an unsustainable system more tolerable. They cannot make it aligned.

Alignment requires questioning the premise that owner-occupied homes belong in the tax base at all. That question cannot be answered through appeals or hearings. It requires legislative reconsideration.

The chapters ahead move from diagnosis toward direction. If fixing the process cannot fix the problem, then the problem must be addressed at its source.

What the Homeowner Experiences in Real Life

For most homeowners, the property tax system is not encountered as a policy framework or a legal theory. It appears in far more ordinary ways. It arrives in envelopes, in revised escrow statements, and in notices that seem routine until they no longer are. The language is formal. The deadlines are fixed. The consequences are not optional.

This lived experience matters, because it reveals how abstract design choices translate into daily pressure.

A homeowner usually first encounters the system through a valuation notice. That number reflects market activity that may have little to do with the household itself. Nearby sales, regional growth, investor activity, and broader economic trends all feed into the calculation. None of them change how the homeowner actually lives in the house.

Yet the cost of remaining there increases immediately.

At first, the increase feels manageable. The escrow adjusts. The monthly payment rises modestly. The homeowner absorbs it and moves on. This adjustment feels responsible, even expected.

Then it happens again.

Each year brings a new notice. Each notice reflects accumulated market pressure. Each adjustment narrows the margin a little more. What once felt occasional becomes routine. What once felt minor begins to feel permanent.

This is often when homeowners first engage the appeals process.

Appealing a valuation requires time, attention, and familiarity with procedure. Comparable sales must be identified. Forms must be completed. Deadlines must be met. For some homeowners, this is manageable. For others, it is confusing, intimidating, or simply unrealistic given work schedules, health concerns, or family obligations.

Even when an appeal succeeds, the relief is temporary. The value may be reduced for that year. The following year, the process begins again. Exposure is not eliminated. It is deferred.

Over time, this cycle produces predictable behavior.

Homeowners begin planning defensively. Budgets are built around uncertainty rather than stability. Repairs are postponed because future obligations are unclear. Savings are redirected to cover potential increases. Long-term decisions are approached cautiously.

The home, instead of serving as a stable base, becomes a variable expense.

This experience crosses income levels and life stages.

A retiree on a fixed income may find that rising valuations outpace cost-of-living adjustments. The home they have occupied for decades becomes more expensive to keep, even though nothing about their use of it has changed.

A working family may see modest wage growth while appreciation driven by regional development pushes taxes upward faster. The gap is closed by cutting back elsewhere, often in ways that affect quality of life.

A first-time homeowner may discover that affordability at purchase did not account for ongoing uncertainty. What looked manageable on paper becomes strained as valuation-based increases accumulate.

In each case, the homeowner adjusts to a system that does not adjust to them.

This adjustment is often misunderstood. When homeowners struggle, the explanation is framed in terms of personal budgeting or lifestyle choices. The structural role of the tax system is rarely acknowledged. Burden is individualized. Design remains invisible.

At the center of this experience is an assumption that does not hold up under scrutiny.

The system treats market value as a proxy for capacity. Appreciation is treated as benefit rather than obligation. The distinction between owning an asset and accessing income is blurred. Homeowners are told rising values are good, even when the immediate consequence is higher cost without added liquidity.

This disconnect becomes most visible during periods of disruption.

When income stagnates or declines, property taxes do not adjust automatically. The obligation remains in place until actively reduced through appeal or exemption. The responsibility for alignment falls on the homeowner, not the system.

Over time, that responsibility becomes exhausting.

Homeowners skip appeals. Notices go unanswered. Increases are absorbed reluctantly. Engagement declines not because people stop caring, but because effort never produces lasting stability.

The system continues unchanged.

This experience reshapes how ownership feels. The home no longer feels permanent. It feels conditional on continued financial flexibility. The knowledge that failure carries penalties, interest, and eventual loss—even if rarely realized—changes behavior long before those outcomes occur.

A system does not need to displace large numbers of people to exert pressure. The possibility alone is enough.

This is how structural pressure works. It influences decisions quietly, year after year, without dramatic moments. It narrows options. It shortens planning horizons. It teaches caution where confidence once lived.

The homeowner's experience reveals something essential. The property tax system does more than collect revenue. It shapes behavior. It influences how people plan, spend, invest, and participate.

When that influence undermines stability, the system works against the foundation it depends on.

The chapters that follow step back from individual experience and examine the broader consequences of this design—how reliance on valuation-based taxation of owner-occupied homes affects communities, economies, and the long-term health of the system itself.

Fee Simple Title, Collateral, and the Hidden Contract

Homeownership in America rests on a legal concept so familiar that most people never think to question it. Fee simple title is commonly described as the highest form of property ownership recognized by law. It conveys the right to possess, use, exclude others from, and transfer property freely and indefinitely.

Most homeowners believe they understand this. They believe, quite reasonably, that they own their home.

What is far less understood is how that ownership is conditioned, leveraged, and constrained by the property tax system that surrounds it.

Fee simple title does not exist in isolation. It exists within a framework of obligations that attach automatically and continuously. Among those obligations, property taxation stands apart. It does not depend on use. It does not depend on income. It does not require ongoing consent. It arises solely because ownership exists.

This distinction matters more than it first appears.

When a homeowner signs a mortgage, the obligation is explicit. The terms are disclosed. Payments are agreed upon. Default carries defined consequences. The relationship is contractual, and both sides understand the risk.

Property taxation operates differently. The obligation is not negotiated. It is imposed. It adjusts unilaterally. The homeowner does not reconsent each year. Ownership itself is treated as consent.

This creates what can fairly be described as a hidden contract.

Under this arrangement, the homeowner holds fee simple title in form, but that title is perpetually encumbered by a lien that arises automatically and renews indefinitely. The lien does not wait for delinquency to exist. It does not require notice to attach. It exists by operation of law.

In practical terms, the title is conditional—not in theory, but in lived reality.

This is where collateral enters the picture.

In lending, collateral is pledged to secure performance. The borrower understands the risk. The lender accepts the asset as assurance. The terms are defined, and the obligation is finite.

In property taxation, the home itself functions as collateral for public finance. The homeowner effectively co-signs for obligations incurred by local governments, regardless of whether they participated in those decisions or benefited equally from the outcomes.

This is not rhetorical framing. It is legal reality.

If property taxes are not paid, the home can ultimately be seized and sold. This enforcement mechanism is not symbolic. It is essential to the system's credibility. Without it, the obligation would lose its force.

The fact that seizure is rare does not make it irrelevant. The existence of enforcement shapes behavior long before it is ever used.

This reality quietly alters the meaning of fee simple ownership. The homeowner owns the property, but only so long as they remain able to satisfy an obligation that is externally determined and subject to escalation.

That escalation is not tied to the homeowner's income, health, or stage of life. It is tied to market conditions and budgetary decisions beyond the homeowner's control.

This arrangement might be less troubling if property taxes functioned like a usage fee. They do not.

They function as a revenue engine linked to asset value.

As long as values rise and budgets expand, the obligation grows. The homeowner's equity, rather than serving solely as a store of wealth and security, becomes a basis for ongoing extraction.

This is why collateral is the correct lens.

The home is not merely taxed. It is pledged.

This pledge is rarely acknowledged because it conflicts with how ownership is culturally understood. Americans are taught that homeownership represents independence, stability, and personal security. The property tax system quietly repurposes that security into leverage.

The implications extend well beyond individual households.

When owner-occupied homes serve as collateral for local government spending, the middle class becomes the stabilizing force behind public finance. Their homes underwrite services, debt, and operations.

This may appear efficient. It is also fragile.

Collateral is meant to be diversified and resilient. Concentrating reliance on owner-occupied housing ties public finance to the financial capacity of households whose primary asset is also their shelter. When pressure increases, households adjust first.

They reduce consumption. They defer maintenance. They delay mobility. These adjustments ripple outward into local economies and communities.

At scale, this dynamic weakens the very base the system depends on.

The system assumes that appreciation represents capacity. In reality, appreciation often represents exposure.

A homeowner can be asset-rich and cash-poor. Their home may increase in value while their income remains flat. Treating that increase as taxable capacity ignores liquidity constraints that are both real and widespread.

This mismatch is not accidental. It is structural.

Fee simple title was never intended to function as an open-ended pledge for public spending. Historically, property taxation existed in a very different economic environment, one with different expectations about mobility, wealth accumulation, and household risk.

As housing became the primary vehicle for middle-class stability and retirement security, the consequences of this structure intensified.

The home is no longer just shelter. It represents long-term planning, family continuity, and generational transfer. Burdening it with perpetual, adjustable obligation undermines those functions.

This is why understanding fee simple title matters.

It is not an abstract legal concept. It defines the boundary between ownership and obligation. When that boundary erodes, ownership becomes conditional in practice, even if it remains absolute in name.

This chapter establishes a foundational truth.

If the home is pledged as collateral for public finance, then protecting homeownership requires revisiting that pledge itself. Appeals, caps, and exemptions do not address the pledge. They merely soften its terms.

Structural reform requires questioning whether owner-occupied homes should serve this role at all.

The chapters ahead build on this premise. They examine the economic, social, and political consequences of maintaining the current arrangement—and why legislative action at the state level is not only appropriate, but unavoidable.

When the Foundation Weakens, Everything Above It Shakes

Every structure depends on the strength of what supports it. When the foundation is solid, stress is absorbed and distributed. When it weakens, pressure migrates upward and outward, often in ways that are not immediately visible.

The American property tax system now rests heavily on owner-occupied housing. This reliance did not arrive suddenly or through a single decision. It grew gradually, quietly, and without a clear moment of consent. Over time, it became normal.

The consequences of that reliance are no longer subtle.

When the home is treated as collateral for local government finance, household stability becomes inseparable from budget stability. This connection functions smoothly only when economic conditions are favorable. When conditions tighten, strain appears quickly.

Homeowners respond in predictable ways. They reduce discretionary spending. They postpone repairs. They hesitate to relocate. They conserve liquidity because the future feels less certain.

Each of these decisions makes sense at the household level. Taken together, they produce broader effects.

Reduced spending affects local businesses. Deferred maintenance affects housing quality. Reduced mobility affects labor markets and community renewal. What begins as individual adjustment becomes systemic drag.

These effects are visible in communities across the country.

Areas experiencing rapid appreciation and rising property tax pressure often show slower turnover, increased household stress, and growing resistance to new development. Residents become defensive rather than optimistic. Growth is perceived as threat rather than opportunity.

This reaction is often misunderstood.

Homeowners are not opposed to public services. They are not opposed to investment. They are opposed to unpredictability tied to something they cannot control. The problem is not growth itself. It is growth converted into obligation without regard to timing or capacity.

That conversion creates friction between stability and progress.

Over time, this friction undermines the social contract.

The middle class has long served as the stabilizing force in American society. Predictable expenses, steady employment, and gradual wealth accumulation have supported civic participation and long-term planning. When housing becomes a source of anxiety rather than security, that stabilizing role weakens.

The effects extend beyond economics.

Households under persistent financial pressure participate less. They attend fewer meetings. They engage less in local decision-making. They withdraw not from apathy, but from exhaustion.

The system unintentionally trains its most reliable contributors to disengage.

At the same time, local governments become increasingly dependent on the very households becoming less resilient. Budget commitments made during periods of growth are difficult to reverse. Fixed costs remain fixed even as household flexibility declines.

This creates a feedback loop.

As budgets expand, reliance on property tax revenue deepens. As reliance deepens, pressure on homeowners grows. As pressure grows, household resilience declines. As resilience declines, the tax base becomes more fragile.

This loop is not sustainable.

Attempts to relieve pressure within the loop often fail because they do not interrupt the underlying dependency. Rate adjustments, exemptions, and caps redistribute burden temporarily. They do not reduce reliance.

Over time, these measures complicate the system without strengthening it.

The risk here is not sudden collapse. It is gradual erosion.

Systems rarely fail all at once. They strain, adapt, and strain again until their original purpose becomes secondary to survival. In this case, a system designed to fund local services slowly undermines the households that make those services possible.

The consequences are generational.

When younger households observe instability in ownership, they delay entry or avoid it altogether. When older households fear displacement, they resist change. The ladder that once connected generations weakens.

Ownership becomes less about building and more about holding on.

This chapter is not an argument against local government. It is an argument against over-reliance on a single source of collateral to sustain it. Healthy systems diversify risk. Fragile systems concentrate it.

If owner-occupied homes continue to function as the primary stabilizer for local budgets, the system will increasingly trade long-term social stability for short-term fiscal convenience.

The chapters ahead turn toward alternatives. They examine why legislative action is the appropriate mechanism for change and how redefining the role of owner-occupied housing can restore balance rather than reduce capacity.

Stability is not preserved by squeezing the foundation. It is preserved by strengthening it.

Why the Middle Class Always Pays First

When systems come under strain, they rarely distribute pressure evenly. Instead, they shift it toward what is dependable, predictable, and difficult to escape. This shift is not always deliberate. It is structural.

In the American property tax system, that pressure falls most heavily on the middle-class homeowner.

This is not because the middle class is intentionally targeted. It is because the middle class is reliable. They pay their bills. They comply with rules. They plan ahead. When costs rise, they adjust.

Owner-occupied homes sit at the intersection of responsibility and immobility. Unlike businesses, homeowners cannot easily relocate to reduce exposure. Unlike investors, they are not operating for yield. Unlike renters, they cannot pass costs along.

They are anchored.

From an administrative standpoint, this anchoring makes owner-occupied housing an ideal revenue base. Bills are sent to fixed addresses. Compliance rates are high. Enforcement mechanisms are well established. Revenue arrives consistently.

Reliability, over time, becomes vulnerability.

As budgets expand and alternative funding sources become politically difficult, pressure migrates naturally toward the most stable base. This migration does not require coordination or intent. It follows incentives.

When governments face rising costs, they look first to sources that respond predictably. Owner-occupied homes meet that test.

This is why the burden grows quietly.

Tax rates may rise modestly or remain flat. The real expansion occurs through valuation. Appreciation becomes the vehicle for revenue growth. Homeowners do not vote on appreciation. They do not negotiate it. They experience the result.

This mechanism allows revenue to increase without triggering the same scrutiny as overt tax hikes. The increase feels technical rather than political.

For the homeowner, the impact is identical.

This dynamic disproportionately affects households whose wealth is concentrated in their home. For many middle-class families, the house represents the majority of net worth. It is shelter, savings, and stability combined.

Taxing that asset annually based on market value converts unrealized appreciation into a recurring cash obligation. The benefit exists on paper. The cost arrives in monthly payments.

This is where the imbalance becomes visible.

Higher-income households often have diversified assets and greater liquidity. Lower-income households may qualify for relief programs or exemptions. The middle class frequently falls between these categories.

They earn too much to qualify for meaningful assistance and too little to absorb ongoing increases comfortably.

They are expected to adjust.

Over time, this expectation reshapes behavior. Middle-class homeowners become cautious. They prioritize liquidity over long-term investment. They delay improvements that might increase assessments. They avoid risks that could strengthen communities.

These decisions are rational. They are also corrosive.

When the middle class retreats, community vitality weakens. Local economies depend on stable households willing to invest in place. When that willingness declines, growth becomes uneven and fragile.

Ironically, the system designed to fund local services begins undermining the conditions that make those services sustainable.

The burden also affects civic trust.

Homeowners who feel perpetually squeezed begin to question whether the system serves them at all. They comply because noncompliance is costly, not because the arrangement feels fair.

Compliance without consent slowly erodes legitimacy.

The property tax system relies on voluntary compliance reinforced by enforcement. When compliance becomes defensive rather than participatory, the social contract thins.

This erosion is subtle, but persistent.

The middle class rarely revolts suddenly. They adapt quietly. They make sacrifices privately. They disengage gradually. By the time strain becomes visible, it has often been present for years.

This chapter highlights a central reality.

The property tax system does not merely collect from the middle class. It conditions their behavior. It shapes how they plan, invest, and participate in their communities.

A system that consistently pressures its most stabilizing group eventually destabilizes itself.

The solution is not to demand more resilience from households already carrying the load. It is to reconsider whether owner-occupied homes should continue functioning as the primary shock absorber for public finance.

The next chapter examines how this reliance became normalized—and why alternatives are often dismissed before they are seriously considered.

Why Alternatives Are Always "Impossible"

When discussions turn toward structural reform, the conversation tends to follow a familiar script. Proposals are acknowledged briefly, examined superficially, and then dismissed. The language varies, but the conclusion rarely does.

It can't be done.
It won't work.
There's no alternative.

This reaction is not unique to property taxation, but it is especially pronounced here because the system has come to rely so heavily on owner-occupied housing. What is often framed as impossibility is, in reality, dependence.

The property tax system did not become dominant because it was morally superior or economically neutral. It became dominant because it was administratively convenient and politically durable. Over time, that convenience hardened into reliance.

Reliance, left unexamined, becomes assumption.

Funding schools, infrastructure, and local services through property taxation now feels inevitable because generations have lived entirely within this framework. The question of whether shelter should be taxed at all is treated as radical rather than foundational.

That framing matters.

Alternatives are rarely evaluated on their own merits. They are measured against a system optimized for continuity rather than adaptability. Any proposal that disrupts existing revenue flows is labeled risky before its broader implications are considered.

Risk, however, is already present. It is simply assigned differently.

When owner-occupied homes function as collateral for public finance, households absorb volatility while institutions preserve stability. Alternatives tend to shift some of that responsibility back toward policymakers and public budgeting.

That shift is uncomfortable.

Consider how these conversations typically unfold. A proposal to reduce or eliminate taxation on owner-occupied homes is raised. Almost immediately, attention turns to revenue gaps. Essential services are invoked. Worst-case scenarios are outlined.

What is rarely questioned is the current trajectory.

The assumption embedded in these reactions is that existing spending levels are fixed and beyond reconsideration. Revenue mechanisms are debated. Expenditure growth is treated as immovable.

This asymmetry shapes outcomes.

Alternatives are framed as threats to services rather than opportunities to realign priorities. The possibility that the current system may already be undermining long-term service sustainability is left unexplored.

In this context, "impossible" often becomes shorthand for "politically inconvenient."

From a technical standpoint, alternatives exist. States already fund significant portions of public services through income taxes, consumption taxes, fees, and intergovernmental transfers. The mix varies widely across jurisdictions. No single approach is universal.

The notion that owner-occupied housing must remain in the tax base is not a law of nature. It is a policy choice.

That choice persists because it distributes cost quietly and predictably. Appreciation masks increases. Compliance rates are high. Enforcement is reliable. These features make the system attractive from an administrative standpoint, even as it places growing pressure on households.

When alternatives are dismissed, the costs of maintaining the status quo are rarely included in the calculation. Household instability, reduced mobility, delayed investment, and civic disengagement do not appear on budget spreadsheets.

They are diffuse, long-term, and difficult to quantify. Revenue, by contrast, is immediate and visible.

This imbalance skews decision-making.

Over time, a feedback loop forms. The more the system relies on owner-occupied homes, the more disruptive any alternative appears. The more disruptive alternatives appear, the deeper reliance becomes.

Breaking this loop requires reframing the question.

The issue is not whether alternatives are painless. No funding mechanism is. The issue is where pressure is concentrated and whether that concentration supports or undermines long-term stability.

A system that protects institutional budgets by steadily pressuring households can appear stable for a long time. But stability built on private strain eventually gives way.

Alternatives become "impossible" only when imagination is constrained by existing commitments.

This chapter does not propose a specific replacement mechanism. That discussion comes later. Its purpose is to clear intellectual ground and loosen assumptions that have hardened into reflex.

If reform is to be taken seriously, the premise that owner-occupied homes must serve as perpetual collateral must be questioned openly. Until that happens, every alternative will be dismissed before it is fully considered.

The next chapter turns to where meaningful change can actually occur—and why state-level action is not only appropriate, but necessary.

Where Real Change Actually Happens

By this point in the discussion, one conclusion should be difficult to avoid. The property tax system does not persist because it is optimal, fair, or aligned with modern homeownership. It persists because it is embedded.

Recognizing that shifts the conversation from frustration to strategy.

If owner-occupied homes are functioning as collateral for local government finance, and if that arrangement is producing instability rather than security, then meaningful reform cannot occur at the margins. It cannot be achieved through better notices, refined appeals, or improved procedures. It must occur at the level where the structure itself is authorized.

That level is the state.

This is not a political claim. It is a legal one.

States create property tax systems. They define what is taxable. They establish exemptions. They allocate authority to local governments. Cities, counties, and school districts operate within frameworks they did not design and cannot fundamentally alter.

This distinction matters because it clarifies where effort is most effective.

Local engagement feels intuitive. Homeowners attend appraisal hearings, city council meetings, and school board sessions because those forums are visible and accessible. They also feel responsive. But they are limited.

Local officials cannot remove owner-occupied homes from the tax base. They cannot redefine fee simple ownership. They cannot alter the constitutional or statutory foundations of property taxation.

They can manage within constraints. They cannot rewrite them.

State legislatures, by contrast, possess the authority to reconsider first principles.

They can determine whether shelter should be treated as a taxable asset. They can decide whether owner-occupied homes should continue to function as collateral for public finance. They can redesign funding structures to reflect modern economic realities rather than inherited assumptions.

This kind of reconsideration is not unusual.

States regularly adjust tax policy in response to changing conditions. Income tax brackets shift. Sales tax bases expand or contract. Exemptions are added or removed. Entire funding models evolve as demographics and economies change.

The reluctance to revisit property taxation is cultural as much as fiscal.

Property taxes feel permanent because they are old. But longevity is not proof of suitability. Many long-standing systems have required adjustment when the conditions they were built for no longer existed.

Early property tax frameworks emerged in an era when land ownership correlated more directly with productive capacity. They were not designed for a world in which homeownership serves as the primary vehicle for middle-class stability, retirement security, and long-term planning.

They did not anticipate modern financing structures, valuation volatility, or prolonged income stagnation. They certainly did not envision perpetual extraction driven by appreciation untethered from liquidity.

As a result, modern homeowners operate within a framework that has drifted far from its original context.

State-level reform is the only mechanism capable of correcting that drift.

This does not mean abandoning public services or retreating from shared responsibility. It means aligning funding mechanisms with current realities rather than historical inertia. It means acknowledging that shelter occupies a unique role deserving structural protection.

State action also changes the political dynamic in important ways.

Local reform often places homeowners in opposition to the officials delivering services they value. It personalizes what is actually a structural issue. State-level reform reframes the discussion.

It shifts the focus from "who pays" to "how should we fund."

That shift matters.

As long as owner-occupied homes remain in the tax base, homeowners will continue functioning as silent guarantors of public spending. Their equity will remain exposed. Their stability will remain conditional.

Removing that exposure requires courage because it challenges assumptions that feel settled but are not. It requires a willingness to revisit foundational choices rather than managing their consequences indefinitely.

The chapters ahead turn from where change must occur to what that change could look like. They examine why a 100 percent exemption for owner-occupied homes is not radical, but corrective, and how restoring true fee simple ownership strengthens society rather than weakening it.

This chapter marks the transition.

Up to this point, the focus has been diagnostic. From here forward, the focus becomes directional.

If the home is truly foundational, then protecting it is not optional. It is structural.

Why a 100 Percent Exemption Is Not Radical

At first glance, the idea of a 100 percent exemption for owner-occupied homes can sound extreme. That reaction is understandable, not because the idea is unsound, but because the conversation around property taxation has been framed incorrectly for a long time. The proposal is often described as a giveaway, a loss of revenue, or an abandonment of responsibility.

It is none of those.

A 100 percent exemption for owner-occupied residential property is not a departure from principle. It is a return to one.

The principle is simple. Shelter is not income. It is not production. It is not speculation. It is the physical foundation upon which personal freedom, family stability, and economic participation rest. Treating it as a revenue source equivalent to income or investment confuses ownership with capacity.

Tax systems function best when they respect that distinction.

Historically, property taxes emerged in economic environments where land was directly productive. It generated crops, rents, or extractive value. Taxing that output made sense because the asset itself produced income. Shelter, as such, was not the primary focus.

Over time, that distinction blurred.

As housing markets developed and appreciation became commonplace, value itself became taxable regardless of use. The home shifted quietly from being a place to live into a basis for revenue. This change did not occur through deliberate reassessment. It happened gradually, through convenience and normalization.

The result is the system we have today.

Owner-occupied homes are taxed not because they generate income, but because they exist. Homeowners are expected to convert paper appreciation into cash payments indefinitely. Failure to do so leads to penalties, liens, and eventual loss.

Calling this normal does not make it reasonable.

A 100 percent exemption corrects this misalignment. It recognizes that the home occupies a different category than other forms of property. It removes shelter from the revenue equation without removing responsibility from citizens.

This is where the proposal is often misunderstood.

Exempting owner-occupied homes does not eliminate taxation. It reassigns it. Income remains taxable. Consumption remains taxable. Production and investment remain taxable. Economic activity continues to fund public services.

What changes is the pledge.

The home is no longer treated as collateral for public finance.

This distinction matters more than any short-term revenue projection.

When owner-occupied homes are removed from the tax base, ownership becomes stable by design rather than conditional by enforcement. Families can plan long-term without the persistent fear that decisions made elsewhere will make shelter unaffordable.

That stability produces effects that are often overlooked in fiscal analysis.

Households invest with greater confidence. Maintenance and improvement increase because future costs are predictable. Mobility improves because ownership no longer feels like a trap. Communities benefit from continuity rather than churn.

These outcomes are not theoretical. They are consistent with how people behave when their footing is secure.

Critics often argue that exempting homes merely shifts the burden elsewhere. That is true, and it is the point. The question is not whether burden exists, but whether it aligns with economic reality.

Taxing income taxes income.
Taxing consumption taxes consumption.
Taxing production taxes production.

Taxing shelter taxes existence.

One of these does not belong with the others.

Another common objection is that homeowners benefit from public services and should therefore pay for them directly through property taxes. This argument confuses usage with funding mechanism. Citizens contribute to shared needs in many ways. The question is not whether homeowners should contribute, but how.

When contribution is tied to asset value rather than economic participation, the burden becomes detached from capacity. A retired homeowner pays more because the market changed, not because their use of services increased. A working family does not gain new capacity because appreciation occurred elsewhere.

That disconnect undermines legitimacy.

A 100 percent exemption restores coherence. It affirms that shelter is protected and that responsibility for funding public services is tied to participation in the economy rather than mere possession of a home.

This is not anti-government. It is pro-alignment.

Governments exist to support stable societies. Stable societies depend on secure households. Undermining that security in order to fund the system meant to protect it is circular.

Removing owner-occupied homes from the tax base breaks that loop.

Importantly, this reform does not stand alone. It must be paired with deliberate funding transitions, transparent budgeting, and political accountability. That is not a weakness of the proposal. It is one of its strengths.

When revenue growth is no longer automatic through appreciation, spending must be justified. Priorities must be chosen. Trade-offs must be acknowledged openly.

That is not dysfunction. That is governance.

Resistance to a 100 percent exemption is less about feasibility than adjustment. Systems built on autopilot resist change because change requires decision-making. But decision-making is precisely what public leadership is meant to do.

This chapter establishes the central proposition of the book.

Exempting owner-occupied homes is not radical. Continuing to treat shelter as collateral is.

The chapters that follow address how such a transition could occur, what objections must be answered honestly, and why postponing reform only increases the eventual cost.

The Slow Shift No One Is Watching

Large systems rarely change through dramatic announcements. More often, they evolve quietly, through a series of small adjustments that feel manageable in isolation but significant in accumulation. Pressure builds, discomfort grows, and incremental changes are introduced to relieve immediate strain. Over time, those changes begin to point in a direction, even if no one has formally acknowledged it.

Property taxation is moving through that kind of shift now.

Public frustration with rising property taxes has become increasingly difficult to ignore. Homeowners have spoken clearly enough that lawmakers can no longer dismiss the issue as isolated or temporary. In response, exemptions have expanded. Caps have been adjusted. Messaging has softened. Relief has been offered in measured pieces.

At the same time, something else has been happening quietly.

The taxable base has been narrowing.

This narrowing is typically framed as practical modernization. Business personal property exemptions expand. Thresholds rise. Certain commercial assets are removed from taxation altogether. Each change is justified on its own terms. Compliance costs matter. Economic competitiveness matters. Small businesses face real pressure.

Individually, these arguments are reasonable.

But systems respond to arithmetic, not intent.

When portions of the tax base are removed, the remaining base must absorb more of the load. If owner-occupied homes remain within that base, pressure does not disappear. It consolidates.

This is the risk few are willing to name openly.

As public resistance makes it politically difficult to extract more from homeowners directly, and as organized interests reduce exposure elsewhere, the system adjusts by omission rather than design. Burden shifts quietly, without transparency or deliberate choice.

This creates a dangerous illusion.

It appears that the system is responding to public concern while quietly becoming more fragile. Relief is granted at the margins while the core mechanism remains unchanged. The appearance of reform masks the reality of consolidation.

In effect, the system is buying time.

If this trajectory continues, lawmakers will eventually face a choice they have postponed. Either the remaining tax base absorbs unsustainable pressure, or the structure itself must be reconsidered. Delaying that choice does not make it easier. It makes it more expensive.

There is a reason emergency reform is always harsher than deliberate reform. When options narrow, trade-offs become more severe. Trust erodes faster. Stability is harder to restore once it has been shaken.

Timing matters.

Removing owner-occupied homes from the tax base deliberately and transparently is not avoidance. It is acknowledgment. It recognizes what is already happening and brings it into the open. It replaces quiet drift with intentional design.

A decisive shift clarifies responsibility. It ends the illusion that incremental relief will resolve a structural problem. It forces honest discussion about funding, priorities, and limits—conversations that are unavoidable in any healthy system.

Just as importantly, it restores trust.

Public trust does not require perfect outcomes. It requires coherent ones. When people understand the rules and believe those rules align with reality, compliance follows naturally. When rules feel arbitrary or contradictory, frustration grows even when relief is offered.

Right now, trust is eroding quietly. Homeowners sense that something is off, even if they cannot fully articulate it. They see exemptions expand while obligations persist. They hear assurances while bills continue to rise.

Confusion fills the space where clarity should be.

A system that relies on confusion to function cannot maintain legitimacy indefinitely. Eventually, people stop believing explanations and begin withdrawing in small, defensive ways.

By removing owner-occupied homes from the equation entirely, that noise disappears. The largest source of frustration is resolved cleanly. Public energy shifts from protest to participation. Conflict subsides not because people are appeased, but because the system finally makes sense.

What remains is manageable.

This chapter does not argue that transition is easy. It argues that delay is harder. The slow shift already underway will continue whether it is acknowledged or not. The only real question is whether it will be guided deliberately or allowed to fracture under its own weight.

The next chapter turns to the most common objections to this approach and explains why they persist, even as they fail to resolve the underlying problem.

The Objections That Always Appear—and Why They Fail

Whenever a foundational reform is proposed, the objections arrive quickly and with confidence. They are familiar, well-practiced, and often delivered as though they settle the matter before it has truly begun.

Over time, repetition gives these objections the appearance of authority.

Most of them, however, are incomplete. They rely on assumptions that have gone unexamined for years, and they protect the structure of the existing system more than they protect the public interest. Understanding them matters, not because they should halt reform, but because they reveal what the current system is actually preserving.

The first objection is always about revenue.

The question is usually framed bluntly: how will schools, roads, police, and essential services be funded if owner-occupied homes are removed from the tax base? The implication is that shelter itself is the source of public support and that removing it creates a dangerous void.

This framing misunderstands how public services are funded.

Public services are supported by economic activity. Income, consumption, production, and investment generate the resources governments rely on. Shelter does not produce revenue. It provides stability. It allows people to work, earn, spend, and participate.

Removing owner-occupied homes from the tax base does not eliminate contribution. It removes a misaligned point of extraction.

The second objection centers on fairness.

Critics argue that homeowners benefit from local services and should therefore pay directly through property taxes. On the surface, this sounds reasonable. But it collapses under closer examination.

Citizens contribute to public services regardless of housing status. Renters pay indirectly. Homeowners pay directly and indirectly. Workers pay through income taxes. Consumers pay through sales taxes. Businesses contribute through payroll and production.

The question is not whether homeowners contribute. The question is whether shelter should be the mechanism.

Fairness is not achieved by taxing what is easiest to seize. It is achieved by aligning obligation with capacity and participation. A retired homeowner does not consume more services because their home appreciated. A working family does not gain new capacity because the market shifted.

Taxing shelter based on appreciation confuses benefit with existence.

The third objection focuses on political feasibility.

Even if reform is desirable, critics argue, it cannot pass. Institutions will resist. Voters will oppose it. The system is too entrenched.

History suggests otherwise.

Nearly every significant tax reform was once considered impossible. Income tax adoption, rate restructuring, exemption expansion, and deduction reform all faced intense resistance until inaction became more dangerous than change.

Political feasibility follows clarity. When people understand what is being protected and why, resistance softens. Confusion breeds opposition. Coherence builds consent.

The fourth objection concerns displacement.

Opponents warn that removing owner-occupied homes from the tax base will simply shift the burden onto renters or businesses. This concern deserves serious consideration.

But displacement is already occurring.

As commercial exemptions expand and business personal property thresholds rise, the tax base narrows quietly. The difference is that these shifts occur without transparency or public debate. Burden consolidates not by design, but by default.

A deliberate exemption allows for intentional balancing. It forces honest discussion about where responsibility should rest rather than allowing it to drift invisibly.

The final objection appeals to tradition.

Property taxes have always existed. Homeownership has always carried obligation. This is simply how things work.

Tradition explains longevity. It does not justify continuation.

Systems built for one era do not automatically serve another. The economic conditions under which property taxation emerged bear little resemblance to today's housing economy. Clinging to tradition while ignoring consequence is not conservatism. It is neglect.

Each of these objections shares a common flaw. They treat the current system as the baseline rather than one option among many. They assume continuity is safer than change without measuring the cost of continuity itself.

That cost is already being paid by households whose stability is eroding quietly.

The purpose of this chapter is not to dismiss objections, but to remove their false inevitability. None of them are insurmountable. All of them require honest accounting rather than reflexive defense.

The next chapter turns from argument to responsibility. If reform is necessary and achievable, the remaining question is who must act—and what action looks like.

Responsibility, Citizenship, and the Long View

At some point, every serious argument reaches a crossroads. Diagnosis gives way to responsibility. Awareness brings with it the quiet expectation of response.

This is that point.

Up to now, this book has examined how the property tax system operates, why it persists, and how it quietly undermines the stability it claims to protect. The conclusion is not dramatic, but it is clear. Owner-occupied homes have become collateral for public finance, and that arrangement is no longer sustainable.

Recognizing this creates an obligation—not just for policymakers, but for citizens.

That obligation is often misunderstood.

Responsibility does not require anger. It does not demand constant engagement or ideological alignment. It does not ask every homeowner to become an expert in tax law or public finance.

It asks for clarity.

A system cannot be corrected if it remains unnamed. A problem cannot be addressed if it is continually reframed as something else. For decades, rising property taxes have been treated as administrative annoyances rather than structural signals.

They are signals.

They indicate a system leaning too heavily on its foundation. They reveal a growing disconnect between public finance and household capacity. They warn that stability is being traded, slowly and quietly, for convenience.

Citizenship begins with acknowledging that warning.

For homeowners, this does not mean abandoning local participation. Appeals, hearings, and community involvement still matter. They provide accountability within the structure that exists today. They remain necessary.

But they are not sufficient.

Structural change requires engagement at the level where structure is defined. That level is state governance. It is constitutional. It is statutory. It is deliberate.

This is where the role of the informed homeowner becomes important—not as an activist, but as a stabilizing voice.

The homeowner who understands fee simple title and collateral does not argue emotionally. They argue coherently. They do not ask for relief. They ask for alignment.

They ask simple questions that are difficult to dismiss.

Why is shelter treated as a revenue source rather than a protected foundation?

Why is appreciation taxed without regard to liquidity?

Why is stability penalized while long-term planning is discouraged?

These questions change the tone of debate.

They move discussion away from personalities and toward principles. They replace frustration with clarity. They require policymakers to explain not just how the system operates, but why it should continue to operate this way.

This is how long-term reform begins.

It does not begin with slogans or urgency. It begins with understanding that systems persist until they no longer can, and that the cost of delay is rarely paid by institutions first.

Homeowners do not need to agree on every detail of reform to agree on direction. Direction is enough to begin moving.

A 100 percent exemption for owner-occupied homes is not a policy endpoint. It is a structural correction. It restores the boundary between ownership and obligation. It reasserts what is protected and what is leveraged.

Implementing such reform will take time. It will require transition, compromise, and adaptation. No serious change avoids these realities.

But gradualism should not be confused with avoidance.

The worst outcome is not imperfect reform. It is continued drift until reform is forced under crisis conditions. Crisis reform is always harsher, more divisive, and less thoughtful than deliberate change.

The long view matters.

Societies that preserve freedom do so by protecting foundations, not by extracting from them until they weaken. Homeownership has long been one of those foundations. Treating it as expendable undermines everything built upon it.

This chapter is not a call to action in the conventional sense. It is a call to orientation.

To see clearly.

To speak accurately.

To refuse confusion where clarity is possible.

The final chapter returns to first principles and asks the question that has been present from the beginning: what kind of future is being quietly co-signed today—and what does ownership need to mean if that future is to remain stable.

What We Are Really Deciding

Every system tells a story about what it values. Sometimes that story is written plainly, in statutes and stated principles. More often, it reveals itself quietly, through outcomes that repeat often enough to feel normal. Over time, those outcomes shape expectations, behavior, and belief.

The American property tax system tells such a story, whether we choose to hear it or not.

It tells homeowners that shelter is conditional. It tells families that stability is negotiable. It tells citizens that ownership lasts only so long as obligations set elsewhere remain affordable. These messages are not delivered in speeches or policy papers. They arrive through notices, escrows, assessments, and deadlines. They are enforced not by ideology, but by arithmetic.

Over time, arithmetic shapes belief.

This book has argued that owner-occupied homes have been repurposed as collateral for public finance. That argument is not rhetorical. It is descriptive. The home now secures obligations the homeowner did not individually incur and cannot individually control. This arrangement did not arise from malice. It emerged through convenience, inertia, and long-standing silence.

But outcomes do not care about intent.

When shelter is pledged indefinitely, ownership loses its defining characteristic: permanence. When permanence erodes, planning erodes with it. When planning weakens, the middle class thins. When the middle class thins, everything built upon it becomes less stable. This chain is not theoretical. It is visible in household behavior, community turnover, and the growing anxiety surrounding what ownership actually guarantees.

The decision facing society is not whether to raise or lower a tax rate. It is whether ownership itself will remain foundational or quietly become provisional.

That decision is already being made, incrementally. Each exemption tweak, each valuation adjustment, each quiet narrowing of the tax base is a partial answer offered without addressing the core question. Incrementalism feels safer because it avoids clarity. It allows the system to adapt without explaining itself.

Clarity, however, cannot be postponed forever.

A system that depends on confusion to function eventually loses trust. A system that requires households to absorb perpetual uncertainty eventually exhausts them. What is truly being decided is not merely how public services are funded, but who bears the risk of funding them.

At present, that risk rests disproportionately on homeowners whose primary asset is also their shelter. This is often described as resilience. In reality, it is exposure.

Reclaiming fee simple ownership in substance, not just in name, requires removing owner-occupied homes from that role. A 100 percent exemption is not a symbolic gesture. It is a clear line drawn deliberately and publicly. It says that shelter matters. It says that stability is protected. It says that the home is not collateral.

Such a decision does not weaken society. It strengthens it.

When shelter is secure, households invest with confidence. When households are confident, communities stabilize. When communities stabilize, governments govern from trust rather than dependence. This is not a utopian vision. It is a structural one, grounded in how people behave when the ground beneath them is steady.

There is also a practical reality worth stating plainly. Releasing owner-occupied homes from the role of collateral does not leave government weaker. It leaves it steadier. The revenue contribution of these homes, relative to the total system, is modest. The stability they provide, by contrast, is foundational. When households are secure, communities function better, economic activity becomes more predictable, and public trust deepens. For policymakers, this creates a rare opportunity—one where protecting homeowners strengthens the system they are responsible for stewarding. Choosing alignment over inertia is not a concession. It is a leadership decision that allows everyone involved to win.

Every generation inherits systems shaped by earlier choices. Those systems either support freedom or quietly trade it away for convenience. The property tax system now sits at that crossroads.

Future homeowners will not ask whether the system was well-intentioned. They will ask whether it was corrected once its consequences became clear. They will judge not the complexity of the system, but the honesty of those who maintained it.

This book does not demand urgency for its own sake. It demands honesty. It asks readers to recognize what is already happening, to name it accurately, and to insist that foundational assets remain foundational.

If the home is truly the cornerstone of middle-class life, then protecting it is not radical. It is responsible.

The question is no longer whether reform is possible. The question is whether it will be deliberate or forced, thoughtful or reactive, earned or imposed. That choice does not belong to systems alone.

It belongs to people.

What we are really deciding today is what ownership is meant to mean.

Made in the USA
Coppell, TX
12 February 2026

70836750R00036